EILEEN DIAMOND

·LET'S MAKE MUSIC FUN!·

THE YELLOW SONGBOOK

Introduction

In this volume of **Let's Make Music Fun!** Eileen Diamond has included a colourful selection of familiar and new songs including action songs, part songs, story songs, instrumental songs and rounds, to form a unique library of topical source material suitable for pre-school, Key Stage one and Key Stage two.

Each song is provided with teaching ideas and notes on performance which help to explore and satisfy a whole range of National Curriculum requirements.

To help find the material you require, all the songs have been identified by Key Stage and song type. Piano accompaniments have been simplified and chord symbols have been added.

Children will enjoy singing these catchy songs over and over again. Fun to learn and fun to teach!

Music and text processed by Halstan & Co. Ltd., Amersham, Bucks., England

Cover Design by Paul Clark Designs

Published 1997

Contents

Songs Suitable for Pre-School and Key Stage One ⟍P⟋ ⟍1⟋

Can You Guess? (*Action Song*) ⟍P⟋ ⟍1⟋	6
The Crocodile (*Action Song*) ⟍P⟋ ⟍1⟋	8
The Down-Up Song (*Action Song*) ⟍P⟋ ⟍1⟋	10
Everybody Stamp Your Feet (*Action Song*) ⟍P⟋ ⟍1⟋	(4)
Find A Bin (*Action Song*) ⟍1⟋	12
Hats (*Action Song*) ⟍1⟋	15
Let's All Sing A Happy Song ⟍P⟋ ⟍1⟋	18
Little Wooden Puppet (*Action Song*) ⟍1⟋	34
Morning Song (*Action Song*) ⟍P⟋ ⟍1⟋	20
One To Ten ⟍1⟋	22
Rat-A-Tat-Tat (*Instrumental Song*) ⟍1⟋	26
Tick Tock Goes The Clock (*Instrumental Song*) ⟍1⟋	33
Walking Down The Street (*Instrumental Song*) ⟍1⟋	28

Songs Suitable for Key Stage One and Key Stage Two ⟍1⟋ ⟍2⟋

Bright Star (*Christmas*)	52
Changing Rhythms (*Instrumental Song*)	56
Christmas Lullaby	39
Join In The Chorus And Sing	42
A Musical Sound (*Instrumental Song*)	46
Pass A Sound	50
The Snail (*Instrumental Song*)	36

Songs Suitable for Key Stage Two ⟍2⟋

The Busy Round (*4 Part Round*)	58
A Catchy Song (*Instrumental Song*)	66
Don't Forget Me (*2 Part Round*)	59
It's Nice To Have A Friend	60
Let's Play A Duet (*Instrumental Song*)	64
Music Makers (*Instrumental Song*)	78
Only Time Will Tell (*3 Part Round*)	83
A Round For Christmas Morn (*4 Part Round*)	70
Sing Away (*4 Part Round*)	72
What Is The Weather Doing Today? (*2 Part Round*)	73
When It's Christmas	74

Alphabetical Song Listing

Bright Star	52	Little Wooden Puppet	34
The Busy Round	58	Morning Song	20
Can You Guess?	6	Music Makers	78
A Catchy Song	66	A Musical Sound	46
Changing Rhythms	56	One To Ten	22
Christmas Lullaby	39	Only Time Will Tell (Round)	83
The Crocodile	8	Pass A Sound	50
Don't Forget Me (Round)	59	Rat-A-Tat-Tat	26
The Down-Up Song	10	A Round For Christmas Morn	70
Everybody Stamp Your Feet	4	Sing Away (Round)	72
Find A Bin	12	The Snail	36
Hats	15	Tick Tock Goes The Clock	33
It's Nice To Have A Friend	60	What's The Weather Doing Today? (Round)	73
Join In The Chorus And Sing	42	Walking Down The Street	28
Let's All Sing A Happy Song	18	When It's Christmas	74
Let's Play A Duet	64		

Learning A Round

Each round should be learnt in unison before part singing is attempted. The instrumentation listed for the rounds is only a suggestion and may be varied according to which instruments are available at the time. Although melody instruments are not used in these arrangements, there is no reason why recorders, strings and other 'c' instruments should not be included. If a selection of several rounds are performed in a concert, vary the instrumentation.

Any of the INSTRUMENTAL or VOICE parts may be omitted from the OSTINATO. The rounds may also be sung unaccompanied, in which case it will be necessary to play a starting note. A useful performance plan is as folows:

1. PIANO plays 4 bar OSTINATO once (or 2 bars twice) alone.
2. PERCUSSION INSTRUMENTS join in OSTINATO in turn.
3. VOICES join in the OSTINATO and continue into the round. The round is sung once in unison, then three times in parts.

Key

(A) Action Song

(I) Instrumental Song

(R) Round

(P) Part Song

(S) Song just for singing

▽P̷ Material suitable for pre-school.

▽1̷ Material suitable for key stage one.

▽2̷ Material suitable for key stage two.

4

Everybody Stamp Your Feet!

Words and Music by
Eileen Diamond

Lively and rhythmic

Clap, *(Clap twice)* when you're feel - ing hap - py, Clap, *(Clap twice)* it's a

cat - chy beat. Clap, *(Clap twice)* now you've got the rhy - thm,

Last verse to Coda

Ev - ery - bo - dy stamp your feet! *(Stamp twice)*

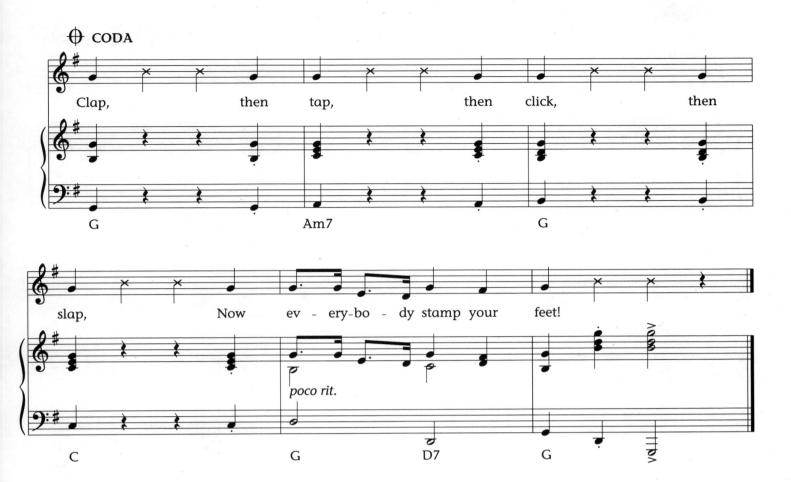

Clap, when you're feeling happy,
Clap, it's a catchy beat.
Clap, now you've got the rhythm,
Everybody stamp your feet.
Clap, then tap, then click, then slap,
Now everybody stamp your feet!

TEACHING IDEAS

A lively, catchy song to help children feel the beat. The varied actions will keep their attention right through to the exciting finish!

Performance

Clap, when you're feeling happy   clap hands
Tap, when you're feeling happy   tap shoulders
Click, when you're feeling happy   click tongues
Slap, when you're feeling happy   slap knees

Each action is performed twice.

Can You Guess?

Words and Music by
Eileen Diamond

Brightly

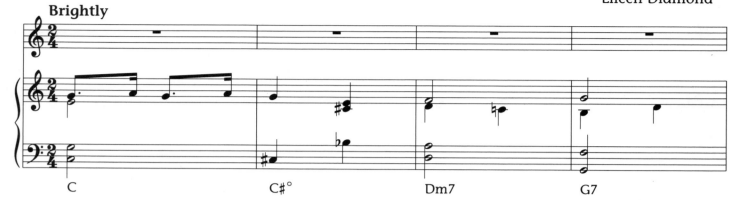

Can you guess what we are? Guess what we're do – ing.

Can you guess what we are, can you guess?

Performing/ playing music

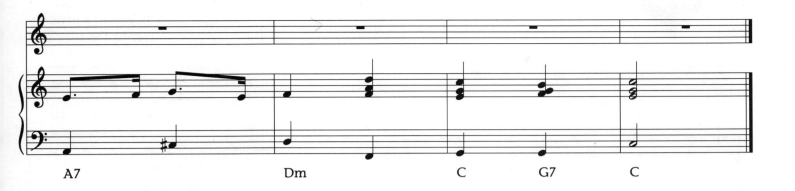

Can you guess what we are?
Guess what we're doing.
Can you guess what we are, can you guess?

 TEACHING IDEAS

A song to encourage listening and observation.

Performance

Divide the children into several groups, then 'secretly' give each group a character or object to mime. Some suggestions are given below, but children may also like to think of ideas themselves. The first group sing the song and when the music plays, they perform their actions. The others watch and then try to guess what they are. The next group has a turn and so on.

Here are a few suggestions:

Elephants, aeroplanes, road sweeper, footballer, violinist, train (holding on, one behind the other), see-saw, trees etc.

Further discussion and development ideas

For a change, this song could be used with musical instruments. Place a selection of any musical instruments behind a screen.

The children sing: Can you guess what we have?
                       Guess what we're playing.
                       Can you guess what we have?
                       Can you guess?

The children then play instruments behind the screen:

Either: 1. Use all the same instruments.
          2. Use two different instruments.
          3. Use three different instruments.

The other children then try to guess which instruments are being played.

The Crocodile

Words and Music by
Eileen Diamond

fish slept in-side all night. Then the croc-o-dile yawned in the

mor-ning light, And the fish swam a-way out of sight.

A crocodile swam in the water,
His jaws were open wide.
A fish swam along in the water
And she swam right inside.

The crocodile's jaws shut tight.
The fish slept inside all night.
Then the crocodile yawned in the morning light,
And the fish swam away out of sight.

TEACHING IDEAS

A short, simple, story-song with actions.

Performance

Place palms together to make crocodile jaws.
Wriggle the fingers of one hand for the fish, then tuck them in tight for when he swims inside.
Snap the palms together for 'The crocodile's jaws shut tight' and then rest head on hands for sleeping fish.
Slowly open palms of hands for crocodile yawning and *wriggle fingers* moving the hand away behind your back for the fish swimming out of sight.

Further discussion and development ideas

For the slightly older children, percussion instruments may be added as an optional extra to create sound effects which enhance the story. For example, a tambourine could be shaken for the crocodile swimming. A scrape on the guiro would be effective for his jaws opening wide. Perhaps sleigh bells gently shaken for the fish swimming, then one drum beat after the word 'Tight' and a ting on the triangle after the word 'Night'. A guiro scrape again for the crocodile yawning and sleigh bells, or even a glissando (slide) up a glockenspiel for the end.

The Down-Up Song

Words and Music by
Eileen Diamond

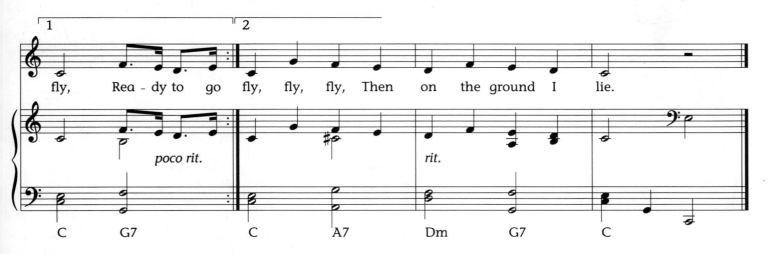

1. Down up, down up, down up,
   This is called the Down-Up Song
   Because we keep on going
   Up when the music goes up;
   Nearly as high as the sky.
   Now hear the music come down again,
   As down and down I fly.

2. Ready to go down up, down up, down up,
   This is called the Down-Up Song
   Because we keep on going
   Up when the music goes up;
   Nearly as high as the sky.
   Now hear the music come down again,
   As down and down I fly, fly, fly,
   Then on the ground I lie.

 TEACHING IDEAS

A song to help children begin to recognise low and high pitch in a fun way, by synchronising body movements with the music and words.

Performance

Down up, down up, down up,
This is called the Down-Up song   bend knees - and up again
Because we keep on going

Up when the music goes up;   stretch arms up high
Nearly as high as the sky.

Now hear the music come down again   bring arms down in flying movement
As down and down I fly,

Ready to go . . .

Repeat song with same actions, then:

. . . then on the ground I lie.   lie down

Further discussion and development ideas

Play a mixture of high and low notes on the piano and tell the children to stretch up high if they hear high notes and bend down low if they hear low notes.

Find A Bin

Words and Music by
Eileen Diamond

Moderate speed, not too fast.

Keep Bri-tain ti-dy,

G7   C G7 C C7

keep Bri-tain clean, Keep Bri-tain just the ni-cest place you've e-ver seen. 1.When you

poco rit.

A7   Dm   G7   C G7 C G7

A little faster

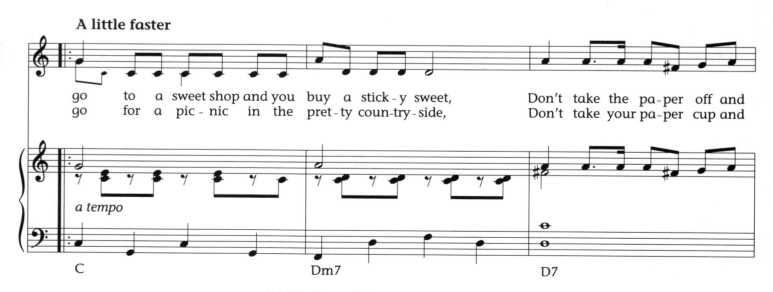

go to a sweet shop and you buy a stick-y sweet, Don't take the pa-per off and
go for a pic-nic in the pret-ty coun-try-side, Don't take your pa-per cup and

a tempo

C   Dm7   D7

Keep Britain tidy, keep Britain clean,
Keep Britain just the nicest place you've ever seen.

1. When you go to a sweet shop and you buy a sticky sweet,
   Don't take the paper off and throw it in the street.

CHORUS:　Find a bin, find a bin,
　　　　　Find a bin and put it in.
　　　　　Find a bin, find a bin,
　　　　　Find a bin and put it in.

2. When you go for a picnic in the pretty countryside,
   Don't take your paper cup and throw it far and wide.

CHORUS:　Find a bin, find a bin, (etc.)

3. When you're stepping off a bus with a ticket in your hand,
   Don't throw it in the road and litter all the land.

CHORUS:　Find a bin, find a bin, (etc.)

4. When you're driving in a car with the windows open wide,
   Don't ever think of throwing anything outside.

CHORUS:　Find a bin, find a bin, (etc.)

 # TEACHING IDEAS

An environmentally friendly song performed in a fun way with actions to really send the message home!

Performance

Choose a few children to play the ♪. ♪♪ rhythm on mixed percussion instruments where indicated. Others may clap the rhythm.

PROPS:　　Waste-paper bin
　　　　　Large, double wrapped lollipop or sweet (so that when the top wrapping is removed, the sweet remains wrapped and is not for eating!)
　　　　　Paper cup
　　　　　Bus ticket
　　　　　Crumpled paper or wrapping from crisps, biscuits etc.

Action:　　Line up four pairs of children and place the waste-paper bin in front of them, centre stage. Give one child from each pair one of the remaining props.

Verse 1:　At the words 'Don't take the paper off and throw it in the street', the first performer unwraps the top layer of the sweet and throws the paper on the floor. The second child picks it up and puts it in the bin.

Verse 2:　The next pair perform similarly. At the appropriate word, the first child throws the cup on the floor and the second child picks it up and puts it in the bin.

Verse 3:　The bus ticket is thrown on the floor.

Verse 4:　One child sits on a chair (or in a toy car if available) pretending to drive. The crumpled paper is thrown out of the 'window'.

Hats

Words and Music by
Eileen Diamond

16

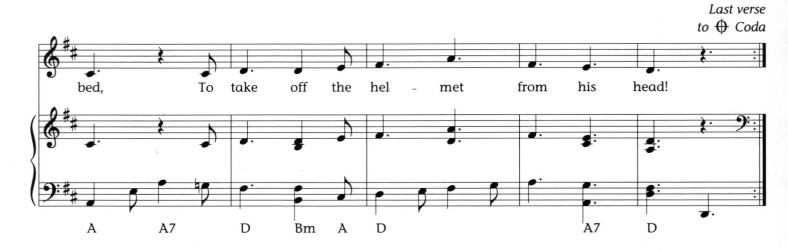

bed,   To take   off   the   hel - met   from   his   head!

A   A7   D   Bm   A   D   A7   D

⊕ CODA

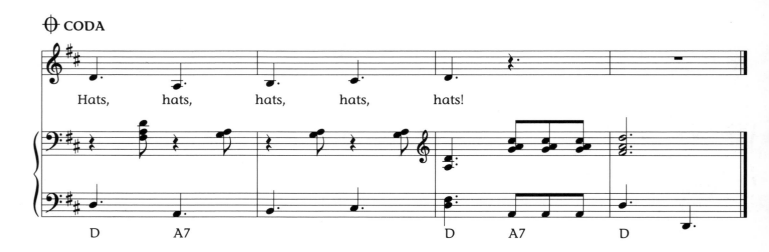

Hats,   hats,   hats,   hats,   hats!

D   A7   D   A7   D

1. Hats, hats, hats, hats,
   Lots of different hats.
   A policeman wears a helmet working on his beat.
   A policeman wears a helmet walking down the street.
   I hope he remembers before he goes to bed,
   To take off the helmet from his head!

2. Hats, hats, hats, hats,
   Lots of different hats.
   A chef wears a tall hat when he goes to bake.
   A chef wears a tall hat when he makes a cake.
   I hope he remembers before he goes to bed,
   To take off the tall hat from his head!

3. Hats, hats, hats, hats,
   Lots of different hats.
   A soldier wears a bearskin to guard the palace wall.
   A soldier wears a bearskin, it makes him very tall.
   I hope he remembers before he goes to bed,
   To take off the bearskin from his head!

4. A queen wears a jewelled crown sitting on her throne,
   A queen wears a jewelled crown sitting there alone.
   I hope she remembers before she goes to bed,
   To take off the jewelled crown from her head!
   Hats, hats, hats, hats, hats!

 # TEACHING IDEAS

A popular, bouncy song that would be visually fun for a concert performance.

Performance

The different hats in the song can easily be made using crêpe paper or oddments. Either one child, or several children (provided there are enough hats) may wear the hats in each verse and perform the following actions:

Policeman	walks up and down
Chef	pretend to stir cake mixture
Soldier	salutes and marches on the spot
Queen	sits on a chair and waves

They remove their hats at the words *take off*.

Further discussion and development ideas

Talk about the different clothes or uniforms people wear for the jobs that they do.

Let's All Sing A Happy Song

Words and Music by
Eileen Diamond

1. Let's all sing a happy song,
    La la la la la, la la la la la la la.
    Let's all sing a happy song,
    La la la la la la la.

2. Let's all hum a happy tune.

3. Let's all see if we can whistle.

4. Let's all clap our hands together.

5. Let's all sing a happy song.

  # TEACHING IDEAS

A happy, participatory song to start the day!

Performance

The children sing, hum, whistle and clap to the rhythm of the song in the appropriate places.
In verse 4, younger children may clap on the beat. Older children may clap the dotted rhythm:

This rhythm may also be picked out in the other verses and played as an accompaniment on percussion instruments if wished. Practise clapping or playing the rhythm a few times first.

Morning Song

Words and Music by
Eileen Diamond

Brightly

1. Wake up and stretch in the morn-ing, Wake up and stretch. Stretch your arms and stretch your bo-dy,
2. Jump out of bed in the morn-ing, Jump out of bed. Throw the cov-ers back so you can

Wake up and stretch. There are lots of things for you to do, Be-fore you start each
Jump out of bed.

day a-new, So wake up and stretch in the morn-ing, Wake up and stretch. school.
jump out of bed in the morn-ing, Jump out of bed.

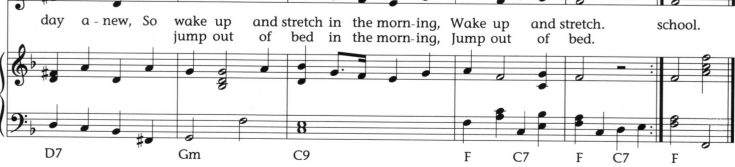

1. Wake up and stretch in the morning,
   Wake up and stretch.
   Stretch your arms and stretch your body,
   Wake up and stretch.

CHORUS: There are lots of things for you to do,
   Before you start each day anew,
   So wake up and stretch in the morning,
   Wake up and stretch.

2. Jump out of bed in the morning,
   Jump out of bed.
   Throw the covers back so you can
   Jump out of bed.

CHORUS: There are lots of things for you to do
   Before you start each day anew,
   So jump out of bed in the morning,
   Jump out of bed.

3. Don't forget to brush your teeth in the morning,
   Don't forget to brush your teeth.
   Up and down and round the sides,
   Don't forget to brush your teeth.

CHORUS:

4. Wash your hands and face in the morning,
   Wash your hands and face.
   Under your chin, behind your ears!
   Wash your hands and face.

CHORUS:

5. Hurry off to school in the morning,
   Hurry off to school.
   Meet your friends and say 'Hello',
   Hurry off to school.

CHORUS:

TEACHING IDEAS

An action song which relates to children's daily activities.

Performance
The children perform appropriate actions while they sing.

Further discussion and development ideas
Talk about their daily routine and what else they might do in the morning, then try composing another verse, using their ideas.

One To Ten

Words and Music by
Eileen Diamond

One, you have just begun,
Two, you're not quite so new.
Three, that's a good age to be,
Four, you know a whole lot more.
Five, you begin to thrive,
Six, you know lots of tricks.
Seven, really feels like heaven,
Eight, what a wonderful state!
Nine, when you're nine, then you feel so much bigger.
It's not long to wait until you reach your first double figure.
And then, and then, and then, you're ten!
Ten, then you're really made
Ten, is a whole decade.
When you're ten years old then you feel just great.
It's a wonderful age to celebrate!

TEACHING IDEAS

A fun song for infants, relating numbers to their ages and stages!

Performance

Make cards with large numbers (1 to 10) on them. Choose ten children and give each one a number card to hold. They step forward in turn as the song is sung, holding up the appropriate number, thus giving a visual concept of quantity.

Practise the spoken words *'and then, and then, and then you're ten!'* starting quietly and getting louder.

The word 'decade' may need explaining.

Further discussion and development ideas

Ask the children for their ideas on what children can do at each stage from one to ten.

Rat-A-Tat-Tat

Words and Music by
Eileen Diamond

Rat-a-tat-tat the

post - man is knock - ing at the door; Rat - a - tat - tat the

post - man is knock - ing there once more. Just a min - ute post - man, I'm

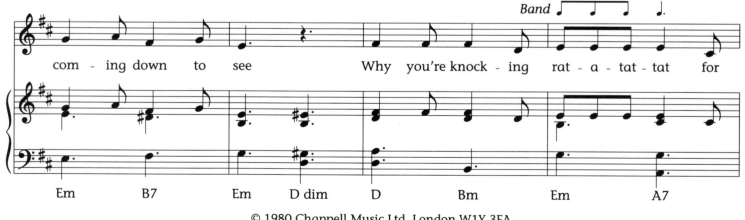

com - ing down to see Why you're knock - ing rat - a - tat - tat for

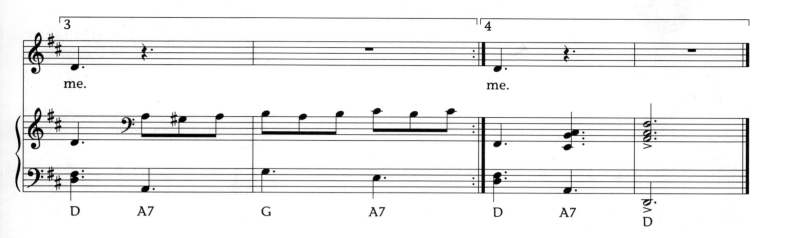

1. Rat-a-tat-tat the postman is knocking at the door,
   Rat-a-tat-tat the postman is knocking there once more.
   Just a minute postman, I'm coming down to see
   Why you're knocking rat-a-tat-tat for me.

   WOOD BLOCKS/
   CLAVES

2. Rat-a-tat-tat the milkman is knocking at the door,
   Rat-a-tat-tat the milkman is knocking there once more.
   Just a minute milkman, I'm coming down to see
   Why you're knocking rat-a-tat-tat for me.

   TAMBOURINES

3. Rat-a-tat-tat the doctor is knocking at the door,
   Rat-a-tat-tat the doctor is knocking there once more.
   Just a minute doctor, I'm coming down to see
   Why you're knocking rat-a-tat-tat for me.

   DRUMS

4. Rat-a-tat-tat the dustman is knocking at the door,
   Rat-a-tat-tat the dustman is knocking there once more.
   Just a minute dustman, I'm coming down to see
   Why you're knocking rat-a-tat-tat for me.

   ALL

TEACHING IDEAS

A jolly song which bounces along with a catchy rhythm and relates to social and environmental experiences.

Performance

Any number of each instrument may be used to play the rat-a-tat-tat rhythm which comes in every verse. Practise playing the rhythm with each group of instruments before starting the song.

Watch out that the children don't start to play at the beginning of the third line 'Just a minute', it's very tempting! They must wait for the 'Rat-a-tat-tat' at the end of the fourth line after the words 'Why you're knocking.'

Further discussion and development ideas

Ask the children to suggest other people who may knock at the door and talk about the different jobs they do.

Walking Down The Street

Words and Music by
Eileen Diamond

1. There was one man walking down the street,
   As he walked along, he played a song.
   Rum tum tum he played on his drum,
   Rum tiddly um tum tum tum tum tum.
   Rum tum tum he played upon his drum,
   Rum tiddly um tum tum.

2. There were two men walking down the street,
   As they walked along, they played a song.
   One went root toot toot on the flute,
   Root toot toot he played upon the flute.
   One went rum tum tum on the drum,
   Rum tiddly um tum tum.

3. There were three men walking down the street,
   As they walked along, they played a song.
   One went ting on the triangle,
   Ting, ting, ting, upon the triangle.
   One went root toot toot etc.
   One went rum tum tum etc.

4. There were four men walking down the street,
   As they walked along, they played a song.
   One went shake on the tambourine,
   Shake, shake, shake, upon the tambourine.
   One went ting etc.
   One went root toot toot etc.
   One went rum tum tum etc.
   Then they all played together, together, together,
   Yes they all played together, walking down the street.

TEACHING IDEAS

This is an accumulative song, stimulating concentration and rhythmic co-ordination.

Performance

Choose four children to play the instruments and line them up ready to play. Everyone sings.

Verse 1:   The first child *'walks down the street'* holding the drum. At the words *'Rum tum tum'*, she/he plays the drum, continuing until the end of the verse.

Verse 2:   The second child joins the first and they walk together. At the words *'Root toot toot'*, she/he plays the recorder (any note) until the drum plays again at the words *'Rum tum tum'*, etc.

Verse 3 & 4: Continuing as verses 1 & 2 with each instrument playing in turn.

Coda: All four walk and play their instruments together on the first and third beats of each bar through to the end. Children without instruments may clap their hands.

Tick-Tock Goes The Clock

Words and Music by
Eileen Diamond

 TEACHING IDEAS

An early-years song for keeping one part going against another and for feeling a steady beat, while at the same time, relating to the children's daily routine.

Performance

Choose one child to play the wood block and another to play the triangle (or chime bar). Divide the other children into two groups. After the two-bar piano introduction, the first group have two bars on their own, whispering or saying quietly 'Tick-tock' repeatedly in eight notes (quavers), accompanied by the wood block.

Then they continue to do this through to the end, against which, the second group sing the words of the song.

At the end of the song, the triangle player decides what the time is going to be and plays that number of chimes while the other children listen carefully (counting silently) and must not call out! The player then asks one of them what the time was and they may all discuss what they might be doing at that time of the day.

When the song is repeated, change over the groups and choose two different children to play the wood block and chimes.

Little Wooden Puppet

Words and Music by
Eileen Diamond

There's a lit - tle wood - en pup - pet and his
name is Bill, When his strings are pulled he just can't keep still; His
feet start tap - ping and his hands start clap - ping And he real - ly can't keep
still, For he's a lit - tle wood - en pup - pet, he can walk a - bout And his

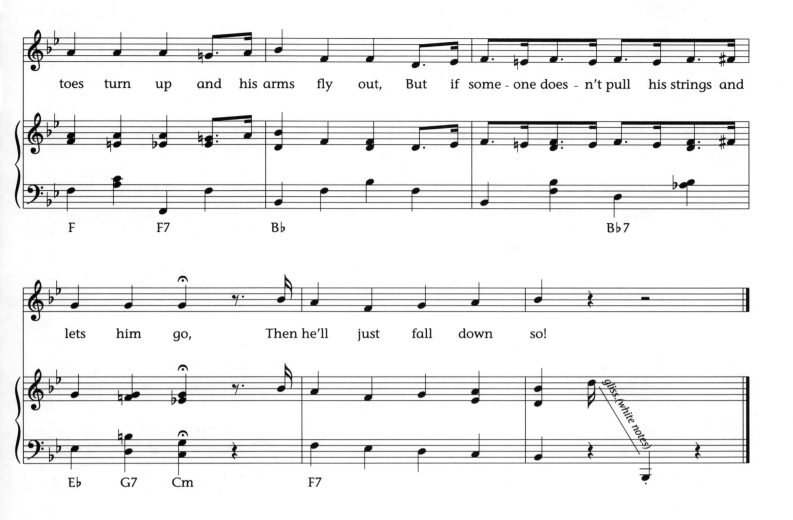

toes turn up and his arms fly out, But if some-one does-n't pull his strings and

F   F7   Bb   Bb7

lets him go, Then he'll just fall down so!

Eb   G7   Cm   F7   gliss. (white notes)

 TEACHING IDEAS

Type of song

A lively action song giving children the opportunity to interpret the movements of a puppet in their own imaginative way.

Performance

Tell the children to imagine that they have strings attached to their hands, feet and head and that someone is pulling the strings to make them move. Then ask them what would happen if someone stopped pulling the strings and let them go! Let them practise these movements freely before singing the song. Perhaps a toy puppet may be available for them to actually see.

The children perform puppet-like actions according to the words of the song. When the music pauses on the word 'go', the children drop their arms but do not fall down until the piano plays the descending glissando (slide) after the word 'so!'.

Further development and suggestions

It's fun to repeat the song after playing another glissando, *ascending* this time. Then the children pretend someone is pulling the strings up again and off they go!

The Snail

Words and Music by
Eileen Diamond

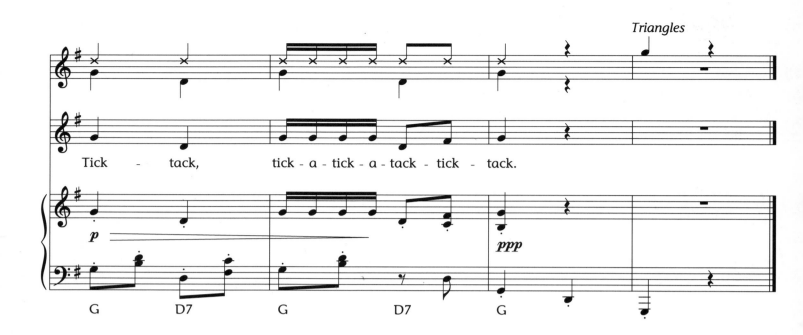

Tick - tack, tick - a - tick - a - tack - tick - tack.

1. Tick-tack tick-a-tick-a-tack,
   Tick-a-tick-a-tack-a-tick tack.
   There's a snail in the garden, see it gliding round the bend.
   It moves very slowly, but it gets there in the end.
   Singing tick-tack, tick-a-tick-a-tack,
   The snail has a house upon its back.
   Tick-tack, tick-a-tick-a-tack.
   It carries its house along.

2. Tick-tack tick-a-tick-a-tack,
   Tick-a-tick-a-tack-tick tack.
   If it hears someone coming, down into its shell it'll hide.
   Then nobody can find it, it's so safe and snug inside.
   Singing tick-tack, tick-a-tick-a-tack,
   The snail has a house upon its back.
   Tick-tack, tick-a-tick-a-tack,
   It carries house along,
   Tick-tack, tick-a-tick-a-tack,
   Tick-tack, tick-a-tick-a-tack,
   Tick-tack, tick-a-tick-a-tack-tick-tack.

 TEACHING IDEAS

A song with a distinctive rhythmic pattern covering the topics of nature and the environment with opportunities for recognising and controlling dynamics.

Performance

The children will easily pick up the catchy 'Tick-tack' chorus in this song. Give the wood blocks and xylophones some practise first and make sure the triangles know when to play. Also, practise the diminuendo (getting quieter) ending. The last 'Tick-tack' should be whispered!

Christmas Lullaby

Words and Music by
Eileen Diamond

There in the low-li-est sta-ble he lay, There by the shep-herds a-dored. Ho-li-est in-fant a-sleep in the hay, Je-sus the son of the

There in the lowliest stable he lay,
There by the shepherds adored.
Holiest infant asleep in the hay,
Jesus the son of the Lord.

So rock him gently,
Rock him gently to sleep.
Saviour of all mankind,
Angels watch will keep.

So rock him gently, etc.

There in the lowliest stable he lay.

TEACHING IDEAS

A quiet and gentle lullaby that would contrast well with a bright and merry Christmas song in a concert programme.

Performance

Practise singing the repeat of the second half of the song quieter and then the final phrase at the end of the song, slower and fading away (diminuendo) to the end.

Join In The Chorus And Sing

Words and Music by
Eileen Diamond

Join in the chor-us and sing. La la la la___ la la la,

La la la la___ la la la, Join in the chor-us and sing.

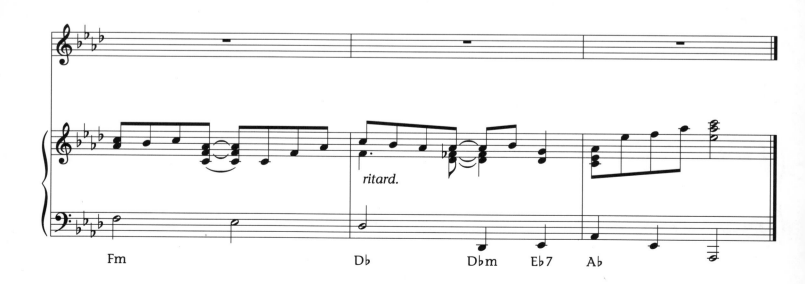

ritard.

Chorus: La la la la la la la
                La la la la la la la
                Join in the chorus and sing,
                La la la la la la la
                La la la la la la la
                Join in the chorus and sing.

1. If there's a song on your mind and you suddenly find
   That you can't remember anything,
   When it begins to go wrong and the words don't belong,
   Just join in the chorus and sing.

   CHORUS

2. Now there is nothing that's worse than a song with a verse
   Having words which carry on and on,
   So just remember that birds never need any words,
   They join in the chorus and sing.

 TEACHING IDEAS

A rousing, catchy, 'Join-in-right-away' chorus opens this song which is suitable for top infants as well as Key Stage 2 pupils.

A Musical Sound

Words and Music by
Eileen Diamond

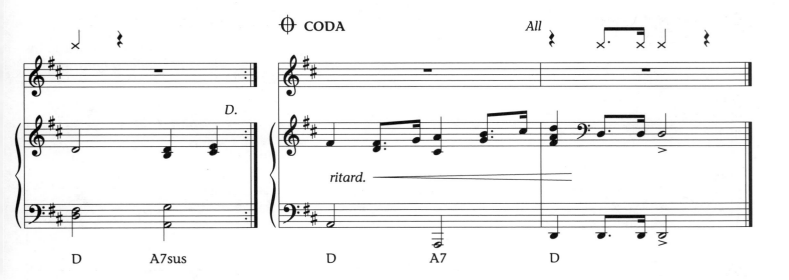

1. When you play on the drums, on the drums, it sounds like this,
When you play on the drums, on the drums, it sounds like this,
And it's good to know you've found
How to make a musical sound,
When you play on the drums, on the drums, it sounds like this.

2. When you play on the shakers, the shakers sound like this, . . .

3. When you play on the bells, on the bells it sounds like this, . . .

4. When you play on the claves, on the claves it sounds like this, . . .

 # TEACHING IDEAS

A song using a number of percussion instruments. Each verse introduces a different group of like instruments to play a simple rhythm at a given moment. A repeated chorus between the verses is accompanied by tambourines and/or children without instruments, clapping.

Performance

If using tuned instruments such as xylophones or chime bars, be sure to play a note compatible with the harmony. The following would be suitable:

1st entry	Play E
2nd entry	Play A
3rd entry	Play F♯
Coda	Play D (or F♯)

Further discussion and development ideas

This song is about making a musical sound. Discuss the difference between a musical sound and noise. This provides a good opportunity to demonstrate the correct holding, playing and general care of instruments and thus avoid their misuse, as well as obtaining the best sound from them. e.g. glocks, xylophones and metallophones should be lightly struck in the centre of each bar. When removing the bars of these instruments, always use two hands and lift them off vertically to avoid damage to the pins. Claves should be played by laying one stick, supported at one end by the thumb and forefinger, across the upturned, cupped palm of a hand (making a sound box). This is struck by the other clave held lightly in the other hand.

Experiment with different tone levels on all instruments, from very quiet through to loud. Also play the xylophones etc. with a variety of beaters such as wooden, felt or plastic and hear which produces the most suitable tone for the song. When the song is known, the children may like to make up some different rhythms for each solo group to play.

Pass A Sound

Words and Music by
Eileen Diamond

Pass a sound a-round the cir-cle, Slap or clap or sing or play.

Pass a sound a-round the cir-cle, Ca-ro-line you can start to-day.

Pass a sound around the circle,
Slap or clap or sing or play.
Pass a sound around the circle,
Caroline you can start today.

 # TEACHING IDEAS

A useful lesson on 'Sound awareness'.

Performance

Although a piano accompaniment is provided, once it is known, this song is equally effective if sung unaccompanied.

Sit in a circle with a few percussion instruments placed in the middle.

The children take turns at thinking of a sound to pass on. Decide who is to start and in which direction the sound will travel round the circle. Then, after singing the song through, the first person sings or plays a 'sound' and each child in turn copies it (if an instrument is used, it is passed from one child to the next) until it reaches the person who started. The song is repeated and a new person starts off a 'sound'.

It is not as easy as it may seem! Concentration and listening skills need to be constantly focused to keep the continuity going without a break.

Any sounds may be used, for example:

Vocal: e.g. One note or more sung to 'la', 'mmm', 'bzz' etc., or a combination of any of these or others, including long and short sounds.

Body: e.g. Clap hands, snap fingers, knock on floor, tap hands on chest, slap knees, or again, a combination of any of these.

Percussion: e.g. Drum, triangle, tambourine, which may be played in different ways: triangle may be struck slowly or rapidly 'tremolo'. Tambourine may be tapped or shaken.

Sounds may be loud or quiet or a combination of both.

Further discussion and development ideas

Get the children to experiment with different ways of making sounds on instruments and also with different levels of singing and playing.

42 bto.

Memory Song 1.

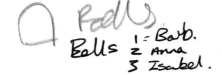
Bells 1 = Barb.
2 Anna
3 Isabel.

Bright Star

Words and Music by
Eileen Diamond

Rhythmically, but not too fast

1. Bright star, ___ ho - ly star, ___
2. Shep - herds ___ left their sheep, ___

Gleam - ing with light ___ on that won - der - ful night ___ Guid - ing wise men ___
An - gels had told ___ them to go and be - hold ___ Ba - by Je - sus ___

On a spe - cial jour - - ney.
Ly - ing in a man - - ger.

1. Bright star, holy star,
   Gleaming with light on that wonderful night
   Guiding wise men on a special journey.

   ×2

2. Shepherds left their sheep,
   Angels had told them to go and behold
   Baby Jesus lying in a manger.

   ×2

   Sing out his praise with triumphant voices!
   Sing out his praise for the world rejoices!
   Jesus born in Bethlehem.

   ×2

   Walk in his ways he was kind and caring.
   Walk in his ways always loving, sharing,
   Jesus born in Bethlehem.

   Bright star, holy star.
   Bright star, holy star.

 # TEACHING IDEAS

A good song for listening skills and control of vocal dynamics.

Performance

Keep the first two verses steady, feeling the syncopated rhythms. Lift the tone for the middle section, let it sound triumphant.

Then bring it down again for a gentle ending, gradually fading away.

Changing Rhythms

Words and Music by
Eileen Diamond

Precisely

Let's play a rhy - thm.

C　G　Am　C　G7　C　Em　F　G

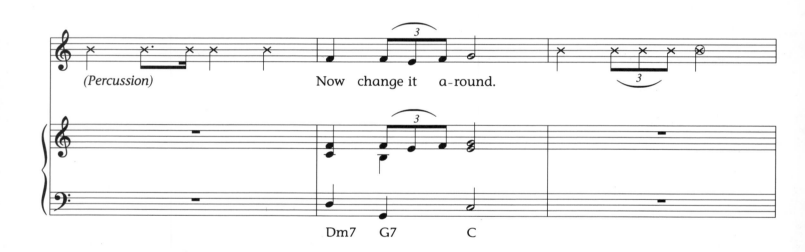

(Percussion)　Now change it a-round.

Dm7　G7　C

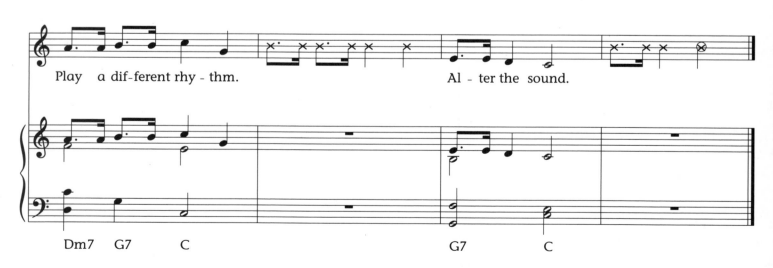

Play a dif-ferent rhy - thm.　Al - ter the sound.

Dm7　G7　C　G7　C

Let's play a rhythm.
Now change it around.
Play a different rhythm.
Alter the sound.

 # TEACHING IDEAS

A short, useful song for imitating and recalling simple rhythmic patterns.

Performance

The rhythms may be played on any percussion instruments, or for variation, try clapping, slapping knees, or tapping feet and sing accordingly:

Let's clap a rhythm . . .

Let's slap a rhythm . . .

Let's tap a rhythm . . .

Further discussion and development ideas

The children may like to try the following:
Keep the melody, but vary the rhythms and if necessary adapt the words to fit. For example:

After some practise at this, the children may be able to compose their own rhythmic variations to fit in with the song.

The Busy Round
(4 part round)

Words and Music by
Eileen Diamond

Brightly

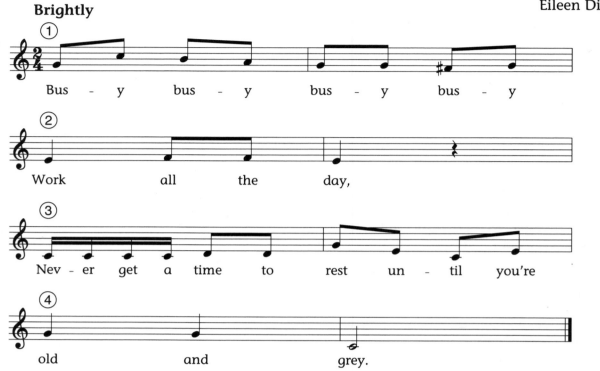

① Bus - y bus - y bus - y bus - y

② Work all the day,

③ Nev - er get a time to rest un - til you're

④ old and grey.

Accompaniment Ostinato

Glocks

Tambourines — No time for a rest, No time for a rest.

Voices — Work all day, Work all day.

Piano

C G7 C7 C G7 C

Don't Forget Me
(2 part round)

Words and Music by
Eileen Diamond

Brightly – with humour

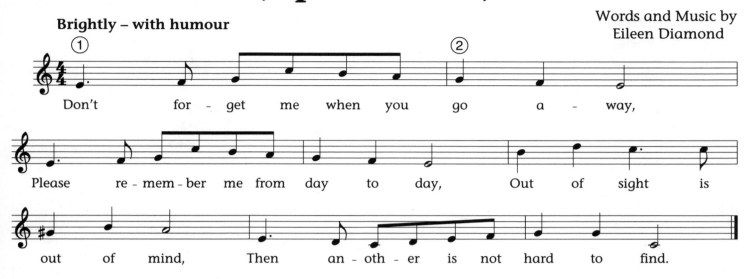

Don't for-get me when you go a - way,

Please re-mem-ber me from day to day, Out of sight is

out of mind, Then an-oth-er is not hard to find.

Accompaniment

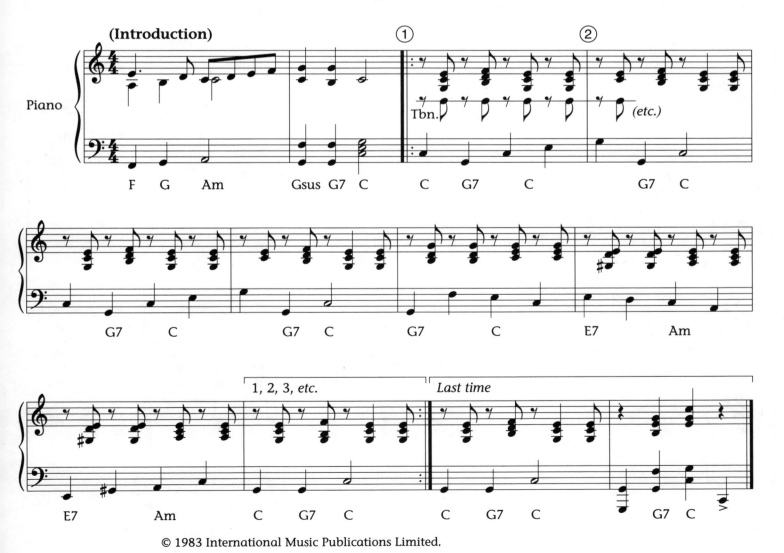

It's Nice To Have A Friend

Words and Music by
Eileen Diamond

Cheerfully

Oh, it's nice to have a friend who you can tell your trou-bles to,

A friend to share the good times and to see the bad times through.

1. To cel - e - brate your hap - pi - ness,___ con -
2. In France you'd have a grand a - mi ___ to
3. In Ger - man - y you'd want to go ___ and

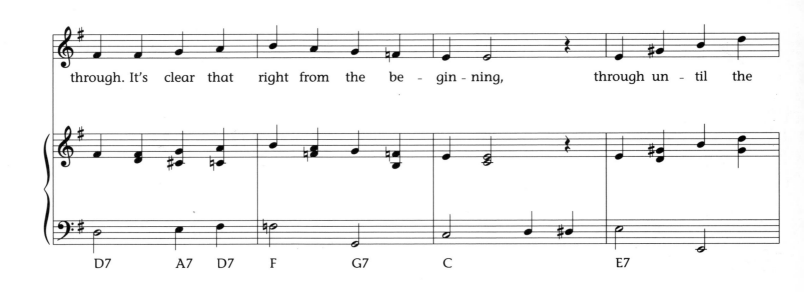

through. It's clear that   right from the   be - gin - ning,   through un - til   the

D7   A7   D7   F   G7   C   E7

end,   Life is   so   much   bet - ter with   a   friend,   Life is

Am   D7sus D7   G   Bm   Dm   C   Cm

so   much   bet - ter with   a   friend. _____

ritard.

G   Gm Am   D7sus D7   G   Em   Am7   D7   G   G6

Oh, it's nice to have a friend who you can tell your troubles to,
A friend to share the good rimes and to see the bad times through.

1. To celebrate you happiness, console you when you're sad.
It makes the good things nicer, and the bad things not so bad.
Oh, it's so nice to have a friend etc.

2. In France you'd have a grand ami to keep you company.
In Spain your gran amigo likes to go wherever you go.

Oh, it's so nice to have a friend etc.

3. In Germany you'd want to go and see your sehr gut freund.
In Italy your amico would be with you every week.

Oh! it's so nice to have a friend etc.

It's clear that right from the beginning, through until the end,
Life is so much better with a friend,
Life is so much better with a friend.

TEACHING IDEAS

A cheerful, straightforward song just for singing

Performance
Before learning the song, ask the children for their views on friendship and what it means to them.

'Friend' in other countries: France - ami, Germany - freund, Spain - amigo, Italy - amico.

Further discussion and development ideas
Do the children know the word for 'friend' in any other languages?

Let's Play A Duet

Words and Music by
Eileen Diamond

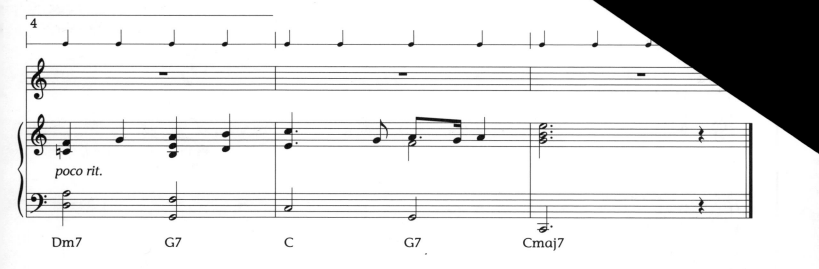

1. Let's play a duet, let's play a duet,
   A duet's for two so that's what we'll do,
   Let us sit down together
   And make lovely music for two.

2. Let's play a trio, let's play a trio,
   A trio's for three, who'll join you and me?
   Then we'll sit down together
   And make lovely music for three.

3. Let's play a quartet, let's play a quartet,
   A quartet's for four so we'll need one more,
   Then we'll sit down together
   And make lovely music for four.

4. Let's play a quintet, let's play a quintet,
   A quintet's for five so one more arrive,
   Then we'll sit down together
   And make lovely music for five.

 # TEACHING IDEAS

An instrumental song beginning with two instruments (duet) and building up to five (quintet). Good practise for listening skills and for thinking about texture and timbre in ensemble playing.

Performance

A piano accompaniment is provided, but this song may be performed using any tuned instruments which the teacher and children are able to play. For a simpler version, the piano or guitar, with any classroom percussion instruments may be used.

Place four chairs next to the teacher and line up four players with their instruments ready to play.

The teacher starts playing her/his choice of instrument and everyone sings the first verse. At the words 'Sit down together', the first child sits down and plays a duet with the teacher, starting from where 'Ensemble' is indicated on the score. If a tuned instrument is used, she/he may either play the top, melody line or may improvise within the harmonic framework. If untuned percussion instruments are used, the players play in steady crotchet beats as indicated.

The song proceeds with everyone singing and two instrumentalists playing, who are then joined by the third player to make a trio and so on, until the song ends with a quintet playing.

Further discussion and development ideas

Ask the children if they know the names for the following:

6 players . . . sextet, 7 players . . . septet, 8 players . . . octet, 9 players . . . nonet.

Listen to some recorded chamber music and see if the children can tell how many instruments are playing and if they can name any of them. Also, ask some children to play a number of different instruments behind a screen, then ask the others to say how many and if possible what kind of instruments were playing.

A Catchy Song

Words and Music by
Eileen Diamond

1. Cym   Dr   SB
2. Sh   Rec   Tgl

1. Crash!   Bang!   Ring, ring, ring,
2. Shake!   Blow!   Ting-a-ling-a-ling,

A7   D   Em A7 D   D   G   D

This is a cat-chy song to sing.   Crash!   Bang!   Ring, ring, ring,
                                   Shake!   Blow!   Ting-a-ling-a-ling,

A7   D   E7   A   D   G   B7

Claves

This is a cat-chy song to sing. You can tap your feet as you feel the beat, You can

Em A7   D   Bm   Em A7   D D7   G   A7   D   D#°

1. Crash! Bang! Ring, ring, ring,
   This is a catchy song to sing.
   Crash! Bang! Ring, ring, ring,
   This is a catchy song to sing.

   You can tap your feet as you feel the beat,
   You can clap your hands in time,
   Cymbals clang! Drums go bang!
   Now sing another rhyme.

2. Shake! Blow! Ting-a-ling-a-ling,
   This is a catchy song to sing.
   Shake! Blow! Ting-a-ling-a-ling,
   This is a catchy song to sing.

   You can tap your feet etc.

3. Tap, scrape, ding, dong, ding,
   This is a catchy song to sing.
   Tap, scrape, ding, dong, ding,
   This is a catchy song to sing.

   Crash! Bang! Ring, ring, ring,
   Shake! Blow! Ting-a-ling-a-ling.
   Tap, scrape, dong, ding, dong!
   This is the end of a catchy song!

TEACHING IDEAS

A song which gives percussion instruments precise moments to play, encouraging concentration and co-ordination. The players really need to be alert in order to play at the right moment and keep it all crisp and in time. It's great fun to perform!

Performance

INSTRUMENTS:

Verse 1: CYMBALS, DRUMS, SLEIGH BELLS
Verse 2: SHAKERS, RECORDERS, TRIANGLES
Verse 3: TAMBOURINES, GUIROS, METALLOPHONES/GLOCKS (B, G, A) and CLAVES for the refrain in between verses.

Children without instruments may tap feet and clap hands in rhythm with the claves during the refrain.

Distribute a reasonable number of each instrument and group the children according to their instrument.

A silent count of 'One, two' on the pause will help them to come in at the same time.

Watch out for 'DONG, DING, DONG' instead of 'DING, DONG, DING' at the end.

A Round For Christmas Morn
(4 part round)

Words and Music by
Eileen Diamond

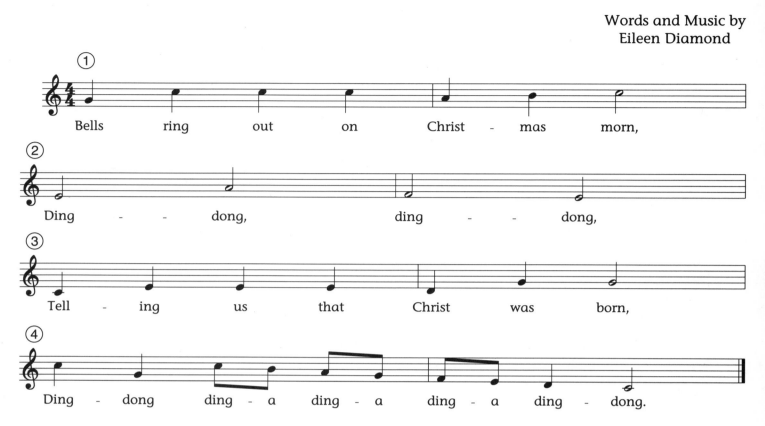

① Bells ring out on Christ - mas morn,

② Ding - - dong, ding - - dong,

③ Tell - ing us that Christ was born,

④ Ding - dong ding - a ding - a ding - a ding - dong.

Accompaniment Ostinato

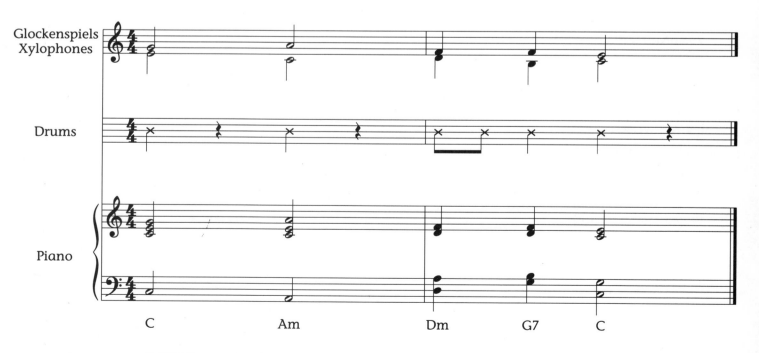

Glockenspiels
Xylophones

Drums

Piano

C   Am   Dm   G7   C

Bells ring out on Christmas morn,
Ding-dong, ding-dong,
Telling us that Christ was born,
Ding-dong ding-a ding-a ding-a ding-dong.

TEACHING IDEAS

A four-part round with ostinato accompaniment.

Performance

Learn the round first in unison until it is secure, before dividing into parts. Also, practise each instrumental part on its own before playing them together.

The following performance suggestion may be useful:

Piano plays 2 bar introduction
Glockenspiels and xylophones join in for next 2 bars
Drum joins in for a further 2 bars
Full ostinato continues while the round is sung once in unison, then three times through in parts
Keep the drum beats fairly quiet

The children may like to compose and add another percussion part for the ostinato.

The round may also be sung unaccompanied after giving a starting note.

Sing Away (4 part round) ▽2

Words and Music by
Eileen Diamond

Lively

① It's good to sing in the morn - ing,

② It's good to sing through the day,

③ It's good to sing when the sun goes down,

④ Sing a - way, sing a - way.

Accompaniment Ostinato

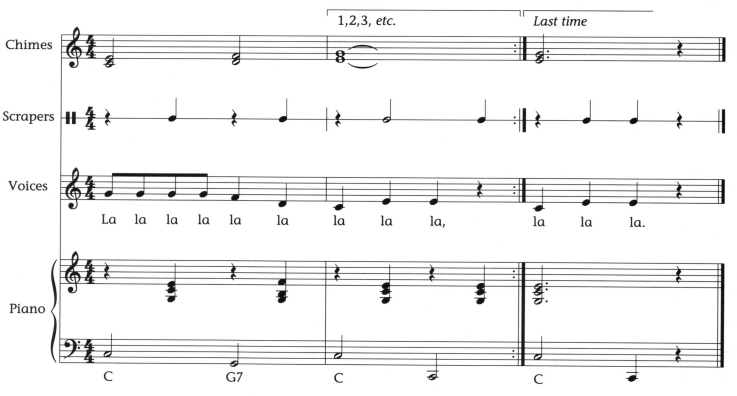

Chimes

Scrapers

Voices — La la la la la la la la la, la la la.

Piano — C G7 C C

What Is The Weather Doing Today?
(2 part round)

Not too fast

Words and Music by
Eileen Diamond

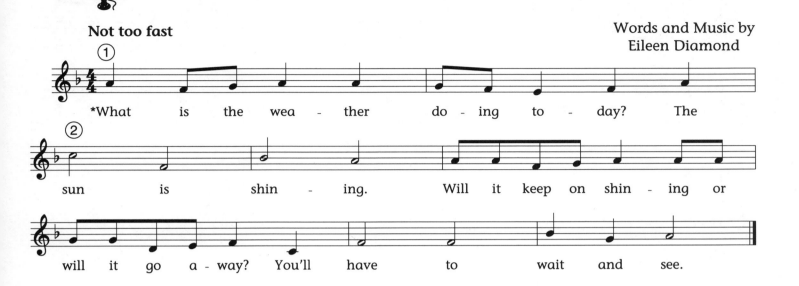

*What is the wea - ther do - ing to - day? The
sun is shin - ing. Will it keep on shin - ing or
will it go a - way? You'll have to wait and see.

Accompaniment Ostinato

Glocks (need B♭)

Triangles

Voices — Mm. — Mm.

Piano

F   Dm   Gm   C7   F   F   Dm   Gm   C7   F

* Alternative verses:

The rain is pouring. (Will it keep on pouring?)
The wind is blowing. (Will it keep on blowing?)
It's cold and snowing. (Will it keep on snowing?)
It's dull and cloudy. (Will it stay all cloudy?)

* Children may also like to make up their own verses.

This round also makes a useful, short song for young children if sung in unison.

When It's Christmas

Words and Music by
Eileen Diamond

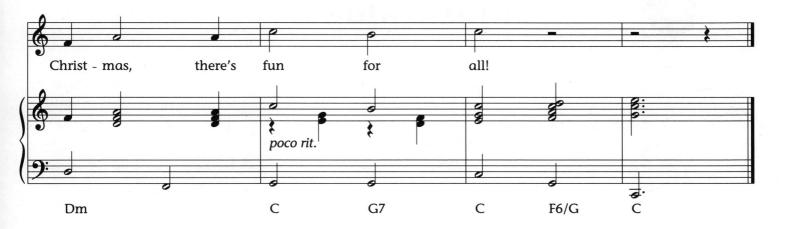

Christ - mas, there's fun for all!

poco rit.

Dm   C   G7   C   F6/G   C

1. When it's Christmas, it's time to go carol singing,
   Listen to the church bells ringing,
   Happiest season, happiest reason,
   When it's Christmas, it's time to go celebrating,
   Christmas tree decorating,
   Join in the Christmas fun.
   It's the season of goodwill to all mankind
   And peace throughout the land,
   It's the season to love, live, laugh, give,
   Lend a helping hand.

2. When it's Christmas, it's time to be feeling jolly,
   Hang mistletoe and holly,
   Happiest season, happiest reason,
   When it's Christmas, then nobody minds the weather,
   Families get together, friends and neighbours call.
   When it's Christmas, there's fun for all!

TEACHING IDEAS

A bright and happy Christmas song which would make a good concert item.

Music Makers

Words and Music by
Eileen Diamond

Brightly, with spirit

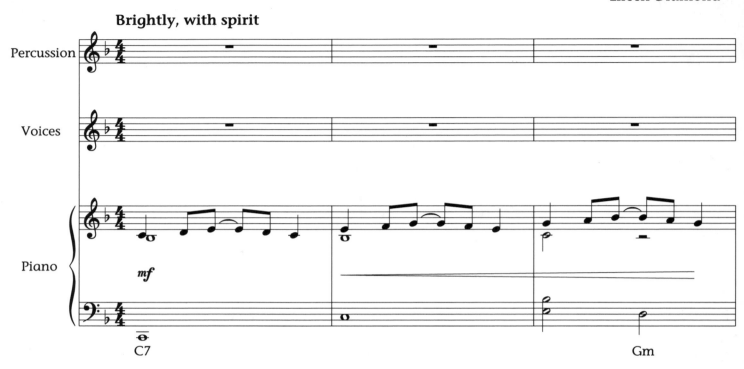

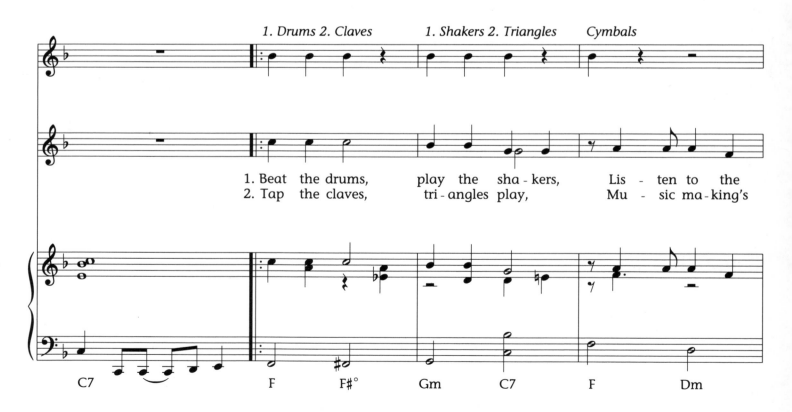

1. Beat the drums, play the sha - kers, Lis - ten to the
2. Tap the claves, tri - angles play, Mu - sic ma - king's

80

1. Beat the drums, play the shakers,
   Listen to the music makers.
   Music making is fun.

2. Tap the claves, triangles play,
   Music making's here to stay.
   Music making is fun.

   Make up a rhythm,
   Play it on the tambourine.
   Other instruments play that rhythm.

3. Guiros scrape, sleigh bells jingle,
   Music makes your senses tingle.
   Music making is fun.
   Music making is fun.

TEACHING IDEAS

A song to encourage listening, a sense of rhythm and improvisational skills. Groups of percussion instruments have specific moments to play. A short passage of rhythmic improvisation is incorporated.

Performance

The percussion players will need to listen carefully so that they come in together on their first beat and cymbal players to listen out for their exact moment to play.

Choose one child to make up the tambourine rhythm in the song before starting. Other instruments may be used as a change to the tambourine e.g. 'Play it on a big bass drum', 'Play it on a pair of claves', 'Play it on a wooden block' etc.

Instruments

DRUMS, SHAKERS, CLAVES, TRIANGLES, CYMBALS, METALLOPHONES/GLOCKENSPIELS, GUIROS, SLEIGH BELLS, TAMBOURINE.

The only notes required on the METALLOPHONES/GLOCKS are F, G, A. The other bars may be removed.

N.B. When removing or replacing bars on these instruments, always use two hands and move them vertically up or down with care to avoid bending the pins which hold them in place.

Further discussion and development ideas

Give the children some practise at playing two-bar rhythms in $\frac{4}{4}$ time.

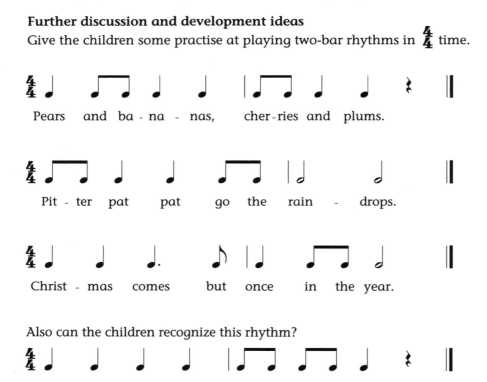

Also can the children recognize this rhythm?

Only Time Will Tell
(3 part round)

Words and Music by
Eileen Diamond

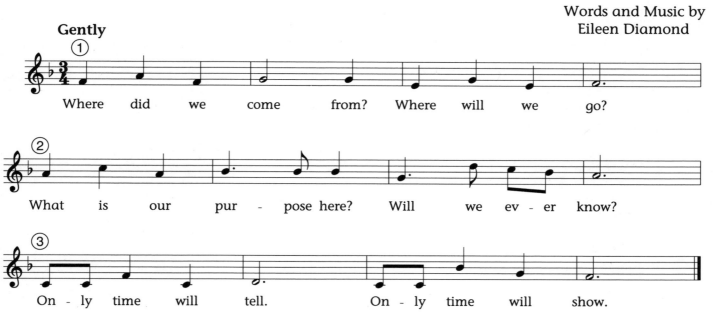

Where did we come from? Where will we go?

What is our pur - pose here? Will we ev - er know?

On - ly time will tell. On - ly time will show.

Accompaniment Ostinato

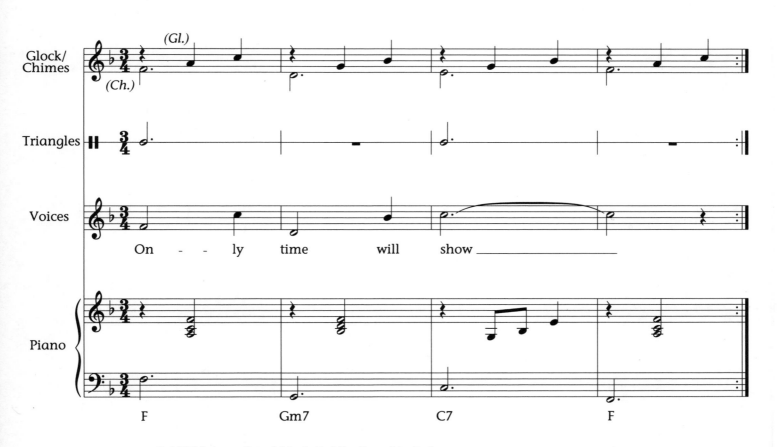

On - ly time will show _____